WILDLIFE IN DANGER

Sally Morgan

FRANKLIN WATTS
NEW YORK • LONDON • SYDNEY

First published in 2000 by
Franklin Watts
96 Leonard Street, London
EC2A 4XD

Franklin Watts Australia
14 Mars Road
Lane Cove
NSW 2066

EARTH WATCH: WILDLIFE IN DANGER was produced for
Franklin Watts by Bender Richardson White.
Project Editor: Lionel Bender
Text Editor: Clare Oliver
Designer: Ben White
Picture Researchers: Cathy Stastny and Daniela Marceddu
Media Conversion and Make-up: Mike Weintroub,
MW Graphics, and Clare Oliver
Cover Make-up: Mike Pilley, Pelican Graphics
Production: Kim Richardson

For Franklin Watts:
Series Editor: Sarah Snashall
Art Director: Jonathan Hair
Cover Design: Jason Anscomb

A CIP catalogue record for this book is available from the British
Library.

ISBN 0-7496-3639-4 (Hbk)
ISBN 0-7496-3878-8 (Pbk)

Dewey classification 333.95

Printed at Oriental Press, Dubai, U.A.E.

Picture Credits:
Tony Stone Image: cover main image (Manoi Shah) and pages
5 bottom (Art Wolfe), 14-15 (Jett Britnell), 17 bottom (David
Woodfall), 27 top (Manoi Shah). **Oxford Scientific Films:** cover small
photo (Kjell Sandved) & pages 13 top (Konrad Wothe), 17 top (Colin
Milkins), 18 (John McCammon), 19 (John Downer), 20 (Michael
Leach), 29 bottom (Mark Hamblin). **NHPA:** pages 7 (Nigel J.
Dennis), 9 bottom (Haroldo Palo Jr.), 13 bottom (Rich Kirchner),
21 bottom (David Woodfall), 25 bottom (Andy Rouse). **Ecoscene:**
pages 1 & 23 top (Tom Ennis), 4 (Andrew D. R. Brown), 21 top (Sally
Morgan), 25 top (Anthony Cooper). **Panos Pictures:** pages 23 bottom
(Jean-Léo Dugast), 27 bottom (Arabella Cecil), 29 top (Fred
Hoogervorst). **Environmental Images:** pages 24 (Clive Jones).
Still Pictures: pages 5 top (Fritz Polking), 8 (Compost/Visage), 9 top
(Mark Edwards), 11 (Kevin Schafer), 12 (Thomas D. Mangelsen),
15 top (Thomas Raupach), 26 (Roland Seitre), 27 bottom left (Jorgen
Schytte), 29 top (Ray Pforiner). **Science Photo Library:** page 10 top
right (Jeff Lepore). **Bruce Coleman Ltd:** pages 10 bottom left (Jane
Burton), 15 bottom (Dr. Charles Henneghien), 22 John Cancalosi,
28 (Trevor Barrett).   **Artwork:** Raymond Turvey.

CONTENTS

BIODIVERSITY

Wildlife is found almost everywhere on Earth – in the air, on land, underground and in the water. So far, a million different species (types) of plants and animals have been identified, but there could be ten million new species waiting to be discovered. This great variety of living things is called biodiversity.

Different homes

The place where an animal or plant lives is called its habitat. There are many different habitats, from the tropical forests to deserts and the frozen poles. Each habitat is home to a different group of plants and animals. Some animals and plants have adapted to live only in one particular type of habitat. For example, tigers are found in the rainforests of Asia and penguins are found in the frozen ice of Antarctica.

This meadow in Portugal provides a habitat for many different species of wild flowers, spiders and insects.

The giant panda feeds on bamboo. It is endangered because the bamboo forests in which it lives are being cleared.

On the Ground

To conserve the panda, the Chinese have created forest reserves. These are linked together with natural corridors of trees to allow the pandas to move between them safely.

Under threat

Giraffes and elands drink at a watering hole in the grasslands of Africa. They share this habitat with lions, rhinoceroses, leopards, cheetahs and zebras.

Wildlife is under threat from the increasing numbers of people, expanding industry and the spread of farming. People are using up the Earth's resources, or raw materials, destroying habitats and producing pollution. The environment has been damaged and some plants and animals have disappeared completely from Earth – they have become extinct (died out completely). People have to find ways of saving the world's wildlife before it is too late.

LIVING TOGETHER

Many different plants and animals live together and share the same habitat. They rely on each other for survival.

Food chains

Plants make their own food using sunlight, carbon dioxide gas from the air and water from the ground. Animals get their food by eating plants or other animals.

The links or feeding relationships between plants and various animals is called a food chain. If something happens to an animal in the chain, all of the plants and other animals in the food chain will be affected, too.

Some plants and animals are links in several food chains. For example, a zebra is in the food chain of lions, hyenas and other predators. Interlinked food chains make a food web.

In this food chain, if the lions are killed, the number of zebras will increase. But the extra zebras will use up more grass. They will overgraze the grassland and soon run out of food.

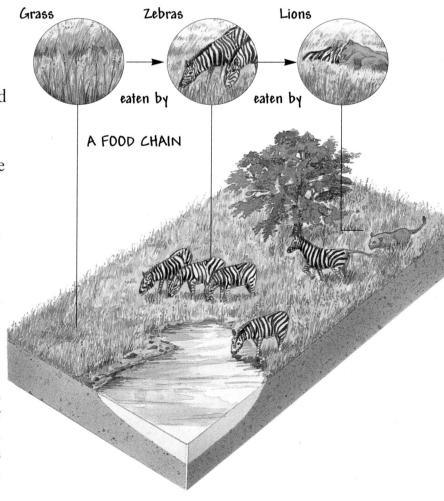

Grass → Zebras → Lions

eaten by   eaten by

A FOOD CHAIN

The bateleur is a type of eagle. It is part of many food chains, feeding on snakes, insects, eggs and the meat of dead animals.

FOOD WEB

A food web consists of a weave of food chains. A habitat, such as the African savannah or grassland, has a large food web. Within food chains, the links start from the animal or plant being eaten.

Disappearing wildlife

The variety of plants and animals on the planet has to be conserved, or saved. This means that habitats have to be protected from major changes and their use must be managed. Since plants and animals rely on each other, it is important to conserve the whole habitat. It is no good trying to protect a single species if its habitat is disappearing.

Sometimes natural events, such as volcanic eruptions or forest fires, threaten or damage a habitat, causing species to become endangered. Today, people's actions create environmental changes that many animals and plants cannot survive. These species are dying out and becoming extinct. Many more species are described as being endangered, because their numbers have fallen to just a few thousand.

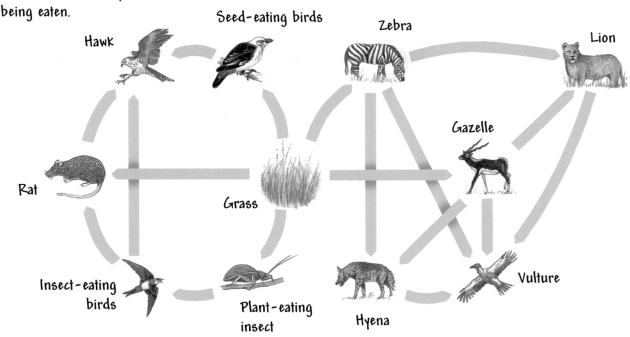

Hawk

Seed-eating birds

Zebra

Lion

Gazelle

Rat

Grass

Vulture

Insect-eating birds

Plant-eating insect

Hyena

RAINFOREST LIFE

Tropical rainforests are found in hot and wet places near the Equator (an imaginary line around the middle of the Earth). These forests only cover one seventeenth of the Earth's surface, but they are home to two-thirds of the world's wildlife.

Unique plants and animals live in the rainforests. The world's biggest flower, rafflesia, grows in the forests of Indonesia.

Rich rainforests

Rainforests have the greatest biodiversity of any habitat. Within a small area there may be hundreds of different trees and birds, and thousands of different insects. This is because the forest contains different conditions and habitats.

Life in layers

The branches of the trees form a roof over the forest. This canopy is rich in food such as leaves, seeds and fruits. Birds, mammals, snakes, frogs and insects make their home in the canopy. The forest floor is dark and damp and covered with fallen leaves and twigs. Small animals, fungi and bacteria live here, breaking down the dead vegetation and recycling it.

This area of the Amazon rainforest in Brazil has been cleared for tin mines. When the trees disappeared, so did the wildlife.

On the Ground

The golden lion tamarin's habitat is rapidly disappearing. Two areas of forests have been made into nature reserves. Any tamarins living in forests which are under threat are caught and moved to the reserves.

The golden lion tamarin, a type of monkey, lives in Brazil's coastal rainforests.

Saving the forests

Already more than half the rainforests have been cleared for timber, farm land, industry and homes. As the trees are cut down, the homes of many animals are destroyed for ever. Once the forests are gone, the land has little value.

Now people are working to conserve the remaining forests. People have to learn how to manage the forests and not threaten wildlife by removing some of the timber, but leaving enough for the future.

NORTHERN FORESTS

Stretching across North America, Europe and Asia is a huge belt of forest known as the boreal forest. The trees are mostly conifers, such as fir, pine and spruce. They can survive the long, cold winters and the short, but warm summers. Boreal forests are home to bison, moose, mountain lions, squirrels and wolves.

Grey wolves hunt in groups of up to 15 animals. Because their prey is scarce, the wolves have to hunt over a huge area to find food.

The barn owl makes its nest in old, hollow trees. It is found in the cold forests of the north.

Eco Thought
The wolf was once a common sight in Europe, but it sometimes attacked animals or even people. The wolf was hunted down until there were none left. Now it is being reintroduced to areas where it once roamed.

Disappearing forests

For a long time, these forests were safe because few people could reach them. But now the trees are being felled for timber, which is used to build homes and furniture and to make paper and match-sticks. In parts of Alaska and Siberia, forests are cleared to make way for oil wells and coal mines. Some forests are cut down to make ski resorts.

Laws now protect parts of the boreal forest but the biggest threat to the forests in Asia is illegal logging. The felling of trees without permission has increased rapidly since the break up of the Soviet Union in 1991. Valuable cedar, elm and ash are smuggled into China, Korea and Japan.

This pipeline is carrying oil across Alaska, in the United States. The oil industry is a serious threat to the survival of the boreal forest.

Planting for the future

Much of the original forest in Scandinavia and North America has been cleared. It has been replaced by managed conifer forests or plantations. Conifer trees are fast-growing and they can be harvested in 50 years.

This type of forest management is sustainable and there will always be a supply of wood in the future. However, the replanted forests are not as rich in wildlife as the old, natural forests. Foresters try to make the new conifer forests more wildlife-friendly by clearing smaller areas and having trees of different ages.

Taking Part

Study a large tree near your home. How many different plants and animals can you find living on it? You may spot mosses, ferns, and strange-looking lichens, which are part-fungus and part-plant. There may be insects or spiders on the leaves and under the bark, and birds and mammals in the branches.

THE FROZEN POLES

Nowhere is as cold and bleak as the North and South Poles in mid-winter. Temperatures may fall as low as -60°C and there is no sunlight. Fierce winds make it feel even colder. Even in the brief summers, temperatures barely rise above freezing (0°C).

Eco Thought

Although Antarctica is completely remote, the seas bring pollution from the rest of the world. This gets into the food chains. Traces of pesticides that are used by farmers thousands of kilometres away have been found in the bodies of penguins.

Surviving the cold

A few animals and plants have adapted to the winds, extreme cold and lack of food. In the Arctic, large furred animals include the polar bear and arctic fox. In the Antarctic, there are penguins with thick feathers to keep them warm. Seals are found at both poles – they have a thick layer of fat that traps their body heat. The polar bear, arctic fox and seal cubs are all hunted for their fur, which is used to make coats and hats.

A mother polar bear with her two cubs.

On the Ground

In 1989, almost 50 million litres of oil spilled from the tanker Exxon Valdez into Alaska's Prince William Sound. The oil spread down the coast, killing 250,000 birds and thousands of marine mammals including seals and sea otters.

Tourists visit Paradise Bay, Antarctica.

Scientists on ice

Until recently, the poles were relatively undisturbed. Today, there are research stations in Antarctica where scientists stay all year. There are new airstrips and fuel stores and more people travelling across the ice on snowmobiles. All the rubbish has to be collected and removed.

Polar tourists

Both poles are becoming popular tourist destinations, too, but visitors must take great care not to damage the fragile polar environment. Discarded rubbish decays slowly. There are only a few plants and they grow extremely slowly. If they are damaged, they take decades to recover.

Digging deep

The rocks under the ice can contain metals, coal and oil. In Alaska and Siberia, the mining and oil industries are very important. There are controls to protect the environment, but there has been pollution from mining. There are probably oil fields beneath Antarctica, too, but in 1991, more than 40 countries signed the Antarctic Treaty, banning any mining in Antarctica for 50 years.

A plane flies in fresh supplies for scientists studying the environment in Antarctica.

OPEN SEAS

More than two-thirds of the Earth's surface is covered by water. Seas and oceans form the marine environment. There are coral reefs, muddy sea floors, deep trenches, shallows and shore lines, each with their own community of plants and animals.

Coral reefs

The coral reefs are home to one-quarter of all marine life and are among the world's most fragile and endangered habitats. The reefs are found in the warm, shallow waters of tropical oceans. They are built by tiny animals called corals which create a habitat for many other animals including fish, lobsters and anemones.

Reefs under threat

Corals need clean, unpolluted water and they are killed by pollution from sewage, fertilizers and other wastes. This affects the rest of the food chains that depend on the coral for their survival.

Local people use dynamite to blow up the coral, which is used as a building material. The most colourful coral-reef fish are caught and sold as aquarium fish. Tourism is also threatening the coral reefs. The reefs are damaged by the anchors of boats and by divers touching the coral animals.

A diver admires a shoal of coral-reef fish, off Fiji. Too many divers break off pieces of reefs for souvenirs.

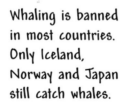

Fishermen in a North Sea trawler haul in the nets. The nets have big holes so that young fish can escape.

Overfishing

Seas and oceans provide people with seafood. However, as the numbers of people increase, more and more fish are caught. Fishing is more hi-tech and trawlers catch whole shoals of fish. Animals such as turtles and dolphins get trapped and die in the nets, too. People are catching far too many fish and too few fish are left behind to breed and produce the new fish.

Marine conservation

Nowadays, many countries limit the amount of fish that can be caught each year. Fishermen have to use nets that allow young fish to escape. Catching whales, known as whaling, has been banned by almost every country in the world. However, the future of the oceans' animals remains uncertain. The seas have been polluted and this affects the health of all marine life.

Whaling is banned in most countries. Only Iceland, Norway and Japan still catch whales.

On the Ground

It's possible to get coral to grow on underwater objects such as old vehicles and planes. These are sunk in shallow areas and within a few years the new coral reef is well-established. These artificial reefs may have an important role to play in the conservation of coral reefs.

15

RIVERS AND PONDS

A healthy river, lake or pond teems with aquatic (water) life such as reeds, rushes, fish, snails and insects. If the water is polluted, all the aquatic plants and animals suffer.

Polluting the water

Many towns and cities have been built on the banks of rivers and lakes, and the wastes from homes and factories have been dumped into the water. The wastes are quickly carried away by water currents, causing pollution along the length of the rivers or all over the lakes.

Harming wildlife

The first animals to suffer are fish, shellfish, frogs and toads and the birds that feed on them. Eventually, only the hardiest plants and animals are left. In many countries, people take water from rivers and lakes for drinking. Water pollution affects them too.

CLEAN AND POLLUTED RIVERS

Clean river

A clean river (left) is home to a wide range of shellfish, fish, birds and insects. Plants grow along its banks. In polluted water (right), only hardy fish and worms survive. A blanket of algae blocks out the sun.

Polluted river

Lack of oxygen

Fertilizers contain chemicals called nutrients that help plants to grow. They are sprayed on crops to make them grow faster and bigger.

Some of the fertilizers drain into streams and rivers, where they add nutrients to the water. Tiny plants in the water, called algae, use these nutrients. The algae grow quickly, creating a thick blanket over the water, cutting out the light to the plants below. When the algae die, they are broken down by bacteria.

The bacteria use up the oxygen in the water, damaging the habitat. As a result, the fish die, which affects the rest of the food chain. The lives of some animals may become threatened.

The water scorpion is a predator. It hunts tiny fish and tadpoles, so it needs unpolluted water to find food.

Taking Part

You can tell if a river's water is polluted by seeing which animals live there. Catch some of the aquatic animals with a net and use a field guide to identify them. Animals that need clean unpolluted water include caddis fly and mayfly larvae, and freshwater shrimps and mussels. Always have an adult close by when you are working near the water.

Ponds are home to a variety of wildlife. Always take care to return any animals you look at.

FARMING AND WILDLIFE

As the number of people increases, more food is needed to feed them. Grasslands, forests and wetlands have all been ploughed up to create farm land.

Machinery saves the farmer time and effort, but it devastates wildlife, such as field mice.

Eco Thought

Sometimes farming helps wildlife. Grazing sheep and cattle stop meadows and grasslands being invaded by brambles, shrubs and trees. As the animals graze, they eat the young shoots of the larger plants and prevent them from growing.

Wildlife deserts

The best farm land in the world – the prairies of North America and the steppes of Russia – were once grassland. Now the grassland has been replaced by huge fields of cereals such as wheat and maize. The largest fields are many kilometres long and wide and have no trees or hedgerows to provide homes for various animals. Such fields are called wildlife deserts because few animals can survive there.

Killing the pests

Pesticides are another threat to wildlife. These are chemicals that farmers use to kill pests that damage crops. Often, pesticides kill wildlife as well as the pests. A bird that eats seeds or insects that have been sprayed with pesticide will also be harmed.

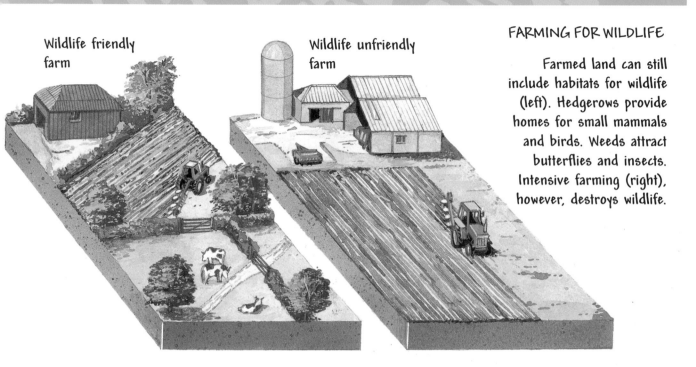

Wildlife friendly farm

Wildlife unfriendly farm

Farmed land can still include habitats for wildlife (left). Hedgerows provide homes for small mammals and birds. Weeds attract butterflies and insects. Intensive farming (right), however, destroys wildlife.

Wildlife-friendly farms

It is possible to encourage wildlife, while still getting good harvests. The corners of fields are too small for machinery to work, so they can be left untouched or 'natural,' or planted with trees to form mini woodlands. Ponds can be dug in damp corners. Natural hedgerows of trees and shrubs can replace barbed-wire fences. Animals such as spiders and birds will eat the pests that damage the crops. If the farmer helps these natural predators to control the pests, there will be no need to use pesticides.

These terraced rice fields in Bali are broken up with occasional trees.

GREEN CITIES

As the human population has grown, towns and cities have expanded. Concrete, glass and tarmac have replaced grasslands and woods, destroying homes for many creatures. But some plants and animals have adapted to living in gardens, parks and city centres.

This pair of white storks have made their nest on top of a church.

Finding new homes

City-centre buildings are tall and packed closely together. This environment attracts birds that prefer high cliffs and ledges. In some cities, people have built special nesting sites for birds such as ospreys, kestrels and storks. Walls have holes and crevices where snails, spiders, woodlice and lizards can hide.

Parks, tree-lined roads and gardens provide shelter and food for birds and squirrels, while garden flowers attract butterflies and other insects. Ponds, rivers and canals bring in herons, frogs, toads and even turtles. Household rubbish in cities provides food for such birds such as crows and such mammals as foxes and racoons.

Taking Part
Sow the seeds of annual flowers such as petunias, stocks, sweet william and candytuft in window boxes or large tubs. These plants produce colourful flowers with scent and nectar that attract butterflies, bees and birds.

Urban pests

Rats and mice have adapted well to the city habitat. They live underground in sewers and drains, feeding on the waste washed down from the streets. In this environment, they breed fast. Unfortunately, they carry many diseases and are a health risk for people. Termites are a pest in tropical cities – armies of them gnaw wood and cause whole buildings to collapse.

Central Park, New York, is a wildlife oasis in the heart of the busy city.

This scrubland just outside Manchester, England, was once the site of a coal mine. It is being replanted and in the future it will become urban woodland.

Wildlife under threat

Every city has areas of derelict land, such as old factories, bomb sites or disused docks. Having been undisturbed for years, these areas have become habitats for many plants, butterflies and birds.

Some of these sites have been made into nature reserves because they are home to a wide diversity of wildlife. As building land in cities becomes scarcer, waste land is cleared for new developments and these important wildlife sites are in danger of being lost.

ANIMAL TROPHIES

Thousand of years ago, our ancestors hunted animals for meat and fur. Hunting still goes on today, but it is no longer primarily to provide essential food or clothing. Instead, animals are hunted for their skin, horns or bones, which are used to make luxury goods.

On the Ground

In Africa, animal conservationists often tranquillize wild rhinos and saw off their horns so that the animals are made worthless to poachers. This is a desperate attempt to save the endangered rhinoceros population.

Ivory and horn

Many animals are protected by law from hunting, but they are still killed by people – usually for money. Illegal hunting is called poaching and it is threatening many endangered animals. The numbers of elephants and rhinos in Africa have fallen to very low numbers in just a few years because of the poaching for their ivory and horn. A ban on the sale of ivory and horn has helped to conserve these animals, but there is a risk that poaching could start again.

A mountain of illegal goods confiscated by customs officers in the United States. It includes carved ivory, painted turtleshells and the skins of big cats.

Fur coats

Animals such as leopards, tigers and lynx are hunted illegally for their skin, which is used to make fur coats. Other animals are hunted and killed because they can be made into tourist souvenirs. Bags and shoes are made from crocodile and snake skin, ornaments are made from attractive shells and jewellery is made from coral.

These rare butterflies and spiders were photographed on sale at a market in Peru.

Orchids that once grew in rainforests are now grown in glass houses for sale in markets.

Collecting plants

It is not just animals that are hunted. People collect rare and endangered plants such as orchids in the rainforests of Asia and cacti in the deserts of the United States. People grow bulbs in their gardens, but they may not realize that some of these bulbs may have been collected from wild habitats.

Stopping the trade

In 1975, CITES – Convention on International Trade in Endangered Species – was set up. Now more than 100 countries have joined this organization, which controls or bans the hunting or trade of those animals and plants that are threatened with extinction. It has successfully stopped most illegal fishing, whaling and the sale of animals furs.

Taking Part
Garden centres have many different types of bulbs on sale. Make sure the label says that the bulbs were grown from cultivated plants and not taken from the wild.

SAVING WILDLIFE

When a species becomes critically endangered, special action needs to be taken to prevent it from becoming extinct.

Looking and learning

So that an endangered animal can be protected, scientists need to know where it lives, what it eats and which predators hunt it. To protect an endangered plant, scientists need to know the type of soil it grows in and whether animals pollinate its flowers. They can then decide whether the species can be protected in its natural habitat or whether it needs to be conserved in a zoo or botanical garden.

On the Ground

Due to hunting and habitat loss there are fewer than 300 Siberian tigers left in the wild. But captive breeding programmes have been successful and there are 300 more in zoos. The next step is to release some tigers back into the wild, but people don't want the tigers released near their homes.

Scientists have injected this lion with a sedative – a drug that makes it drowsy for a few hours. While the animal is sedated, scientists can check its health.

Safety in numbers

Often there may be too few animals left in the wild for males and females to find suitable mates and breed successfully. If there are less than 50 animals remaining, the species is likely to become extinct. Ideally, there must be between 300 and 500 individuals left in the habitat.

Survival in captivity

Sometimes it is possible to set up national parks in which local people can continue to live alongside wildlife but hunting is banned. Failing this, animals can be caught and moved from an area where they are under threat to one which is safe. Or the animals can be moved to a zoo or wildlife park.

At the San Diego Wild Animal Park, endangered species such as the white rhino are protected for the future.

National parks, in which hunting is illegal, protect elephants and other wildlife from poachers.

Captive breeding

When endangered animals breed in a zoo or wildlife park, this is called captive breeding. Zoos can save only a few species, and many animals are not suited to being kept in captivity. The best way is to keep breeding groups in protected areas and after a few years release some of the animals back into their natural habitat. There they can continue to breed and help the survival of the wild population.

On the Ground

Przewalski's horse is the last remaining wild species of horse and it roamed the Gobi Desert of Mongolia. Until the 1990s, this horse was extinct in the wild, surviving only in zoos. By 1992, breeding programmes in zoos had been so successful that a few horses could be reintroduced to Mongolia.

BACK FROM THE BRINK

When there are only a few individuals of a species left, scientists have to plan captive breeding programmes very carefully.

Matchmaking

In a healthy population of animals, individuals show a lot of variation. For example, there may be a range of sizes, colours or eye colour. When there are just a few individuals left, much of this variation has been lost.

Scientists choose the parents of the next generation with care in order to maximize the variation. They try to make sure that animals do not breed with their close relatives. If brothers and sisters are allowed to mate, their offspring tend to be weak and often sterile, which means that they are unable to breed successfully.

In the Philippines, youngsters hold stages in the life of a rare scarlet macaw. The birds are bred for release into the wild.

Eco Thought

Ten per cent of the world's trees are endangered and some have only a few individuals left. Just a quarter of these threatened trees are protected, either in nature reserves, or through cultivation and seed banks.

Animal exchange

Zoos record details of the parents of animals that they keep for breeding. When a zoo is looking for an animal to breed with one of its own, it refers to the records to make sure it does not choose an animal that is too closely related. Zoos sometimes borrow animals from other zoos. For example, giant pandas in captivity are often exchanged for breeding.

This tiger was bred in captivity then returned to a national park, where it is protected by law.

Scientists examine seed bank samples. By collecting genes from hardy seeds, they can breed stronger strains of crops.

Seed banks

Botanical gardens, such as Kew in London, grow large numbers of plants from around the world. However, space limits the number of plants that can be kept. An alternative way to conserve them is to keep banks of seeds. Seeds are collected, dried and stored in freezers. The seeds are tested every few years to check that they will still germinate. If necessary, some of the seeds are germinated and grown into plants from which fresh seeds are collected.

Seeds of all types of plants, not just rare ones, are collected. In the future, these seeds could be used to improve crops or provide new sources of food and medicines.

WHAT CAN WE DO?

Everybody can help to conserve the world's wildlife. Governments can make laws, while individuals can make their local area a better place for wildlife.

At a national park in South Africa, children are taught about animal and plant conservation.

Taking Part

Many local wildlife groups need people to help them conserve wildlife. Volunteers help out on nature reserves by clearing paths, planting new trees and making nesting boxes. Find out if your local wildlife group needs any help.

Taking action

At the Earth Summit in 1992, more than 150 governments signed an agreement to protect the biodiversity of their countries. They agreed to identify the endangered species, describe the threats to these species and explain how they were going to conserve them.

Many countries are now producing action plans. New national parks and nature reserves are being set up to protect wildlife. At the same time, there are laws that make it illegal for anybody to capture, kill or trade in endangered or threatened species.

Volunteers clear up rubbish on a beach in New York, United States.

In Scotland, a badger crossing warns motorists to slow down.

Local wildlife

Everybody can do something to help attract wildlife. An easy way to bring birds into your garden is to put food on a bird table. If you supply a variety of foods, such as nuts, stale bread and fat, you will attract different species of bird. You can also make bird boxes to encourage birds such as blue tits to build nests. Then you can watch the birds lay eggs and raise their family.

Many schools have a wildlife area or garden in the school grounds. Pupils have dug ponds and planted flower meadows to attract different animals. Litter can harm wildlife, so another way to help to protect your local environment is by clearing up any litter dropped in parks.

Watching wildlife

You can learn a lot about animals by watching wildlife in your garden, local park or nature reserve. You can visit local zoos to see what they are doing to conserve wildlife, and you can join organizations that set up national parks.

FACT FILE

Rare cat

The Iberian lynx is the world's most endangered species of cat. It is found in Spain and Portugal where it has been hunted to near-extinction. Reserves have been set up to save the last few lynx.

Saving the ibex

The Himalayan ibex is an endangered goat living in the mountain forests of Pakistan. The Worldwide Fund for Nature has been working with the local people, teaching them how to manage their forests. Now that the ibex's habitat is protected, its numbers have increased to more than 1,000 and its future looks safe.

Fishy business

Soon, people will be able to tell if the fish they buy in supermarkets and fishmongers comes from well-managed fish stocks. Fish caught from managed stocks will be labelled with the sign of the Marine Stewardship Council.

Timber tale

In China there is a ban on logging in some of the most important forests. This will lead to a shortage of timber, so quick-growing tree species have been planted to supply timber for the next 20 years or so.

Conserving coral

The largest marine park in the world protects nearly 2,000 kilometres of the Great Barrier Reef, off the coast of Australia. Some areas are left completely undisturbed, while others are set aside for research, tourism and fishing. The Great Barrier Reef will only survive if other nearby habitats, such as the mangrove swamps and estuaries, are protected as well as the coral reef.

Pet trade

Every year more than 200 million tropical fish are caught on coral reefs and taken to the United States, where they are sold as aquarium fish.

Conserving coral

In the last 30 years, as many as 16 million hectares of coral reefs have been killed. Two-thirds of the world's coral reefs may disappear within the next 30 years.

Polluted lake

The world's deepest lake is Lake Baikal, Siberia, which is 1,485 metres deep. Many of the animals found in the lake, such as the Baikal seal, are found nowhere else in the world. These animals are endangered due to pollution and hunting in the lake.

Seed banks

It is important to protect as many of the world's 250,000 plant species as possible. So far, the seeds of 6,000 species are in seed banks. Kew Gardens in London has the world's largest seed bank. It hopes to have the seeds of 25,000 species of plant safely protected in its seed bank by the year 2010.

GLOSSARY

Algae Tiny aquatic plants.

Aquatic Living in water.

Bacteria Microscopic organisms consisting of a single cell.

Biodiversity The variety of plants and animals.

Boreal forest Forests – mostly of conifers – in the far north.

Captive breeding Mating animals in captivity, for example in a zoo or wildlife park.

Conifer An evergreen tree that has needle-like leaves and bears cones instead of flowers.

Conserve To protect.

Cultivated Grown by people, rather than in the wild.

Deforestation Clearing forests for timber, or to make way for farms, homes or industry.

Endangered Under threat of extinction.

Environment Everything in the surroundings, including plants, animals, rocks, water and air.

Equator An imaginary line around the middle of the Earth.

Extinct Describes an animal. that has completely died out.

Fertilizer Nutrients added to the soil to help plants grow.

Germinate When a seed becomes active and starts to grow.

Habitat Where a plant or animal lives.

Herbivore A plant-eating animal.

Ivory The hard, white material that makes up elephants' tusks.

Nature reserve Land set aside where wildlife is protected.

Nutrients Chemicals needed for healthy plant growth.

Overgrazing When too many animals graze grassland so that no new grass can grow.

Pesticide Substance that will kill insect pests such as greenfly.

Poaching Killing animals that are protected or belong to someone else.

Pollute To poison the air, water or land.

Resources The raw materials – for example, wood, oil, gold – that are used to make things.

Sedative A drug that makes an animal drowsy.

Seed bank A store of frozen seeds.

Shoal A group of fish.

Souvenir Something bought to remind you of your holiday.

Species A particular type of plant or animal. Different species cannot breed together.

Sustainable Able to keep up a way of life or keep resources for a long time.

Trawler A fishing boat.

Tropical The hot, wet regions of the world near the Equator.

INDEX